BRITAIN IN OLD PHOTOGRAPHS

LYE & WOLLESCOTE

A SECOND SELECTION

PAT DUNN

SUTTON PUBLISHING LIMITED

Sutton Publishing Limited
Phoenix Mill · Thrupp · Stroud
Gloucestershire · GL5 2BU

First published 1999

Reprinted 1999

Copyright © Pat Dunn, 1999

Title page photograph: Wollescote Hall.
This is a seventeenth-century house built
on the site of a much earlier one. It was
once the home of the wealthy Milward
family and was briefly the local headquarters of Prince Rupert in the Civil War.
Purchased by industrialist Ernest Stevens
together with its grounds, he presented
them to Lye and Wollescote UDC as a
public park in 1932.

British Library Cataloguing in Publication Data
A catalogue record for this book is available from the
British Library.

ISBN 0-7509-2139-0

Typeset in 10.5/13.5 Photina.
Typesetting and origination by
Sutton Publishing Limited.
Printed in Great Britain by
Redwood Books, Trowbridge, Wiltshire.

THE BLACK COUNTRY SOCIETY

This voluntary society, affiliated to the Civic Trust, was founded
in 1967 as a reaction to the trend of the late 1950s and early 1960s
to amalgamate everything into large units and in the Midlands to
sweep away the area's industrial heritage in the process.

The general aim of the Society is to create interest in the past, present and future of
the Black Country, and early on it campaigned for the establishment of an industrial
museum. In 1975 the Black Country Living Museum was started by Dudley Borough
Council on 26 acres of totally derelict land adjoining the grounds of Dudley Castle. This
has developed into an award-winning museum which attracts over 250,000 visitors
annually.

It was announced in August 1998 that having secured a lottery grant of nearly
£3 million, the Museum Board will be able to authorize the start of work on a
£4.5 million state-of-the-art interpretation centre. This will be known as the 'Rolfe
Street Project', named after the street which once housed the Smethwick Baths. The
façade of this Victorian building is to be incorporated into the new interpretation centre.

At the Black Country Living Museum there is a boat dock fully equipped to restore
narrowboats of wood and iron and different vessels can be seen on the dock throughout
the year. From behind the Bottle and Glass Inn visitors can travel on a canal boat into
Dudley Canal Tunnel, a memorable journey to see spectacular limestone caverns and the
fascinating Castle Mill Basin.

There are 2,500 members of the Black Country Society and all receive the quarterly
magazine *The Blackcountryman*, of which 124 issues have been published since its
founding in 1967. In the whole collection there are some 1,800 authoritative articles on
all aspects of the Black Country by historians, teachers, researchers, students, subject
experts and ordinary folk with an extraordinary story to tell. The whole constitutes a
unique resource about the area and is a mine of information for students and researchers
who frequently refer to it. Many schools and libraries are subscribers. Three thousand
copies of the magazine are printed each quarter. It is non-commercial, and contributors
do not receive payment for their articles.

PO Box 71 · Kingswinford · West Midlands DY6 9YN

CONTENTS

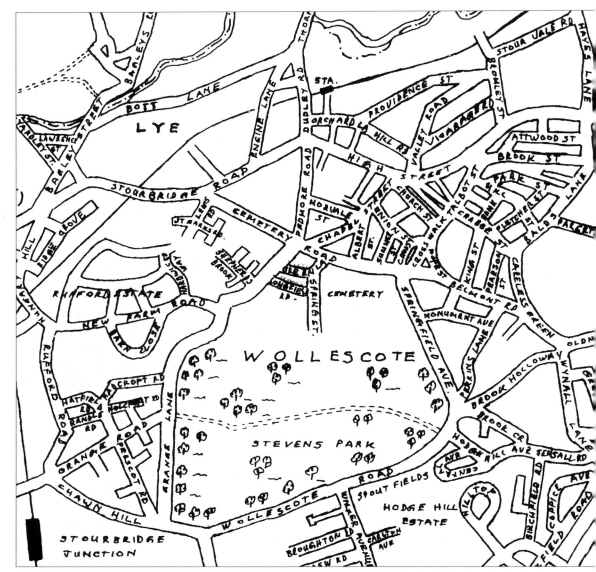

The area covered by this book. Since redevelopment some of the streets have disappeared.

INTRODUCTION

Lye, Wollescote and Stambermill are derivations of Saxon names (pasture, Wulhere's cot and stepping-stone brook mill) but human habitation there goes back much further, with the discovery of Mesolithic and later flints around Foxcote. Worked flints were also found under the foundations of Wollescote Hall, one of the few remaining old houses in Lye. Originally it was a timber-framed building, as was the adjacent Wollescote House, now demolished. Their early occupants would have been engaged in agriculture, but the Milward family at the Hall were industrialists by the time of the Civil War.

The presence of coal, clay and the power of the River Stour, together with easily accessible ironstone, lime and sand, allowed industry to come early here. Coal and clay-mining, brick-making and hand-made nail-making certainly were being carried on by the seventeenth century, as was forging in general. Folkes' Forge is recorded in 1699 and Careless Green House was built at about the same time, together with its adjoining warehouse, by nailmaster Perrins. The now vanished Porridge Hall, home of the Witton family in Pedmore Road, Brocksopp's Hall in Dudley Road and Lye Cross House were other houses occupied by industrialists before the so-called Industrial Revolution.

It was the prosperity of the area with its wealth of coal, clay and ironstone which attracted gypsies to the inhospitable Lye Waste in the 1650s. They eked a precarious living from nail-making, and were Godless and unsociable beings who refused to integrate with their old-established neighbours on the Cross.

William Hudson, the Birmingham historian, wrote in 1780: 'If the curious reader chooses to see a picture of Birmingham in the time of the Britons [i.e. the Celts] he will find one in the turnpike road between Halesowen and Stourbridge called the Lie Waste, alias Mud City. The houses stand in every direction, composed of one large and ill-formed brick scooped into a tenement burnt by the sun and often destroyed by the frost.'

As to the inhabitants, he writes: 'The children at the age of three months take on a singular hue from the sun and the soil which continues for life. We may as well look for the moon in a claypit as for stays and white linen in the city of mud.'

In 1800 Birmingham ministers appealing for funds to build a Congregational church in Lye declared: 'The inhabitants . . . are proverbial in their ignorance and vice. There is no more rude or uncultivated spot in the whole of the British Isles.'

Slowly, however, things began to change, initially through the efforts of the Rev. James Scott, Unitarian Minister of Netherend who opened a chapel on Lye Waste in 1806. In 1813 the Church of England built a chapel of ease (Lye was then still in the ancient parish of Oldswinford) between Waste and Cross, thus helping unify the two disparate communities. Incumbents such as the much-loved Rev. Mr Bromley (1845–66) and his successor Rev. Mr Robertson (1866–75) effected a salutary influence. The latter has left a description of Lye when he arrived there in 1866: 'It was in those days a poor looking place – a place that many would call squalid. The mud huts were much in evidence then. The people building them themselves throwing up balls of mud to the father as he built or repaired the walls. The floors were of clay and the roofs thatched and the crowding was extraordinary. You did not see much of this along the main road but the back streets and courts I must say looked squalid.'

A few years later he was able to report that many of the mud huts had disappeared and new streets with respectable houses had been built; there were a Medical Hall, commercial buildings, Working Men's Institute and Co-operative Society. The manners and habits of the inhabitants had also greatly improved.

The Non-conformists, too, played their part in this metamorphosis. Methodist chapels were built – St John's (1818), Primitive Methodist (1831), Mount Tabor (1871), Bethel (1890), Salem (1893) and Hayes Lane (1896). The Congregational church opened its doors in 1827 and the Salvation Army in 1881.

All the religious groups provided opportunities for education and enlightenment with their own schools or classes. After the 1870 Education Act the state filled the gaps, making education available to all.

Everyday life was always hard and uncertain, but families, friends and neighbours shared problems and helped each other where they could. By the 1840s the domestic hand-made nail trade was in decline and unemployment rife, but other industries were developing – anvil, vice, spade, shovel and chain-making. Local clay was used not only in brick-making, for fireclay also made furnace linings, fire bricks and crucibles. Hollow-ware manufacture was a later arrival, and when galvanising was introduced in 1863 production was so great that Lye became known as 'the Bucket Capital of the world'. Coal-mining went hand in glove with clay-mining, via drift, open cast or small shallow pits.

Eventually factories replaced backyard family workshops, and though these entailed long working hours and dirty conditions they brought discipline and a regular wage-packet. Much of the money earned was spent on drink, for public houses abounded; and gambling on anything under the sun was a major diversion. Cruel sports such as bull, bear, dog and cock fighting as well as bare-knuckle bouts had long been popular. However, as the nineteenth century progressed more seemly entertainments were introduced. Churches and chapels fielded their own football and cricket teams, cultural classes, dramatic and choral productions, and scout and guide troops. The public houses and three political clubs played their part too, with sports teams, bowls, darts, dominoes and pigeon clubs. By the outbreak of the Second World War there were three venues offering public distractions, the Temperance Hall (1874), the Vic (1913), both of which offered live entertainment and film shows, and the Clifton cinema (1937). A purpose-built public library replaced the one-roomed effort in Alton House in 1935, and in 1932 local industrialist Ernest Stevens presented Lye

Stourbridge Road, Stambermill, early 1960s. Bagley Street is on the left and the former Stambermill post office is in the centre. Rufford's weighbridge is on the extreme left.

and Wollescote with a public park. The coming of the railway in 1863 and the trams some thirty years later broadened horizons.

Originally the area had been under the secular jurisdiction of Halesowen, but in 1897 the Lye and Wollescote Urban District Council was created. Until it was disbanded in 1933 and its duties taken on by the borough of Stourbridge it made significant improvements to the local environment, not least by slum clearance, road improvements and public health provisions.

Though the physical appearance changed dramatically some old features of the area remained until the massive redevelopment schemes of the 1960s and '70s, when most local landmarks disappeared for ever. This caused much distress, not least to the Rev. Alan Green, son of Lye's Rating Officer, who had left his home town to become an eminent Congregationalist and respected journalist. In 1957 he wrote an article in *The Times* about the impending changes, and Lye as he had known it in his childhood. 'The Lye [after redevelopment] may have a better layout, modern factories and decent houses,' he wrote, 'but it will not be the town where I was born and I shall look back affectionately to the old place even with its ugliness and squalor.'

For like the novelist, Annie S. Swan, who admired and wrote about the Lye people, he admired them for their independent character, speech and ways. He pointed out that their distinctive dialect, though 'thought by many to be uncouth', was in fact Anglo-Saxon. He cited words such as annunst, meaning near, word-endings like housen (houses), hissen (his), and shoen (shoes), and the declining of the verb to be,

'I bin, thou bist', etc. as pure Saxon. 'Our greeting', he declared, was not 'How are you?' but 'Ow bin yer?' He quoted expressions common in his youth such as dummucked up (tired out), bamboozle (bewilder), chunter (grumble), and slommach (slouch), all of which paint pictures with words.

The Rev. Alan Green also pinpointed another characteristic of Lye – the giving of nicknames to everyone and everything. Often people were not known by their correct surname and nicknames were particularly useful for identifying different families with the same name. Examples of this (from another source) are the Pardoes, who were known variously as Buffer, Apple Pie, Jimmy Ge'it the cat, and Scrape; and the Taylors, who were Bigdick, Billy Boys, Fiddler, Fly, Magic, Old Friend, Pongy, Smacker, Taypot, Tinky, Tizzy, Tracle, Troddy and Wockan.

Alan Green wrote of the Lye characters he had known: there was cattle drover Benny Big Shoes, who so loved music he walked the 12 miles to Birmingham every Boxing Day to hear Handel's *Messiah* – and was usually first in the queue; and Mr Webster of Ye Olde Antique Shoppe in the High Street who did battle with the Council when accused of advertising on his wife's grave. No doubt Lye people today can provide their own examples, and two who immediately spring to mind are Wesley Perrins and Denys Brooks. Both devoted much time and energy to researching and recording the history of the town they loved so well; other Lye-born folk moved away, finding fame and fulfilment elsewhere, for example Cedric Hardwicke, Edwin Morris and Noel Brettell.

Some of them will be found in the pages which follow, as will pictures of the Lye in which they lived, but the book also aims to pay tribute to the unique character of place and people. It will enable readers to 'look back affectionately to the old place even with its ugliness and squalor'.

Stourbridge Road, Stambermill, 1960s. Bagley Street is at the front with the post office on the corner. The white building in the background was the former post office in the early years of the century.

CHAPTER ONE

STREET SCENES

view of Lye Cross, 1890s – when the trams and public lighting were introduced. On the left is the 'Gothick'-style Lye Cross House, birthplace of Hollywood star Cedric Hardwicke. It was then his father's surgery. The cottage on the right was home to Dr Hardwicke's groom.

Lye Cross at the junction of Dudley Road, early 1960s. Lye Cross House still stands, but temporary shops occupy
the site of the adjacent cottages.

Another view of the Cross, 1960s. The temporary shops have gone but Lye Cross House still stands, albeit in
dilapidated condition. It was finally demolished in 1967. Elisha Cartwright's clothing factory, erected on the site
an old building in 1897, is on the far left. This was demolished in 1999. Harvey's tobacconist's and barber's sh
is in the left foreground.

photograph of Centre Cartwright, Elisha's son, born in
905. He was named after the family business premises
nown as Centre Building. This was the first shop in Lye to
ave outdoor electric illumination, which lit up its name at
ight.

he marriage of Elisha's daughter Maud to Harry Carpenter, 8 October 1925. Elisha is standing behind his wife
n the right, next to his son Centre, on his left. Elisha was a miner who studied tailoring at night school and
ecame a prominent Lye businessman. The much-loved Rev. Mr Lewis, Vicar of Stambermill, is on his right. The
ther clergyman is Elisha's son-in-law, Rev. Mr Aston, Vicar of Brockmoor. The young boy is Robert Hill; he sits
ear his parents who are on the extreme left. He became Lye's optician.

Lye Cross at the junction of Pedmore Road, early 1970s. Lye Cross House has gone. The apex of Centre Buildin
can be seen on the left.

A view of Lye Cross, c. 1900. The 'Mericy Bar stands on the left and the ancient Lye Cross Inn, popularly know
as 'Polly Brooks's' is on the right. Both have now disappeared, the former in the 1960s redevelopment scheme an
the latter in the 1930s. Note the various forms of transport and the cobbled street.

The 'Mercy Bar was replaced by new shops in the 1960s redevelopment; they are shown here opposite the 1930s shops which were built on the site of the Lye Cross Inn.

The High Street, early 1920s. Beeton's the newsagent's and bookshop is in the left foreground. Next door is Watkins' butcher's shop adjoining Pig Street (now Clinic Drive), and the Rhodes Buildings beyond stretch into the distance. Opposite may be seen the gateposts of the Congregational chapel, built in 1827.

The High Street looking towards the Cross, early 1970s. The Rhodes Buildings are on the right. On the left is the original Sue Ryder shop, a garage bought by voluntary donations and erected on land given by Mr Gardener of the nearby wine shop. The council replaced it when the road was widened, but it now faces closure through redevelopment.

A scene from the 1928 carnival. It shows the cavalcade passing the Midland Bank, the Misses Hyrams' high-class shoe shop and Freeman's the chemist's. On the far left may be seen the gates of Lye church and the recently erected war memorial. In the centre foreground a collector wears his old army uniform. The float 'Brothflowers' was playing on the name of a contemporary drinkers' club, The Frothblowers.

An advertisement for Freeman's chemist shop, 1937. The wording used is interesting, suggesting that not all chemists were proficient at their job in those days.

The Bank Buildings, late 1950s. The Midland Bank has extended its premises by taking over the adjacent shoe shop. Freeman's is still in business and the Co-operative store trades next door. Car ownership has become commonplace.

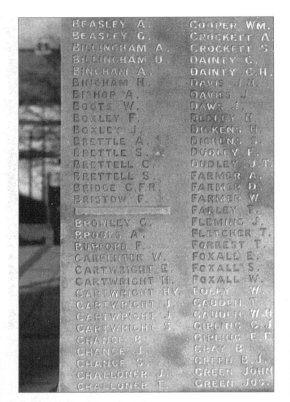

BEASLEY A.	COOPER WM.
BEASLEY G.	CROCKETT A.
BILLINGHAM A.	CROCKETT S.
BILLINGHAM D.	DAINTY C.
BINGHAM A.	DAINTY C.H.
BINGHAM H.	DAVIS J.H.
BISHOP A.	DAVIES J.
BOOTS W.	DAWE J.
BOXLEY F.	DUDLEY H.
BOXLEY J.	DICKENS H.
BRETTLE A.	DICKENS S.
BRETTLE S.	DUDLEY F.
BRETTELL C.	DUDLEY J.T.
BRETTELL S.	FARMER A.
BRIDGE C.F.R.	FARMER D.
BRISTOW F.	FARMER W.
	FARLEY T.
BROMLEY G.	FLEMING J.
BROOKS A.	FLETCHER T.
BURFORD F.	FORREST T.
CARPENTER W.	FOXALL E.
CARTWRIGHT E.	FOXALL S.
CARTWRIGHT H.	FOXALL W.
CARTWRIGHT HY.	FOLEY W.
CARTWRIGHT J.	GADDEN T.
CARTWRIGHT J.	GADDEN W.H.
CARTWRIGHT S.	GIRLING C.J.
CHANCE B.	GIRLING E.F.
CHANCE J.	GRAY B.
CHANCE S.	GREEN B.J.
CHALLONER J.	GREEN JOHN
CHALLONER T.	GREEN JOS.

The war memorial stands in front of the church and was unveiled in 1926 by the local MP, Douglas Pielou. The name F. Bristow, listed among the dead, had to be erased, as he lived for another seventy years and was Borough Librarian for many years after the war.

In the garden of Alton House, family home of the Mobberley family, *c.* 1918. It later became the Council office and library but was demolished to make way for the new library opened in 1935. In the background may be seen the Bank Buildings with the name-board of Hyram's shoe shop partially visible. The occasion for the photograph is unknown but some of those present include Sidney Wassell (end left, back row); in the middle row Elon Harper, -?-, -?-, -?-, -?-, Henry Sidaway, ironmonger, -?-, Harry Brettell, Ernest Sidaway, -?-. Seated, left to right: George Cook, Thomas Hill, Headmaster of the Boys' School, Albert Taylor, -?-, Mr Robins, grocer, -?-, -?-, Cyril Forest, -?-.

The upper High Street, early 1960s. The Clifton cinema is on the right. It would soon yield to the pressure of falling audiences and close. However, when it was built in 1937 it was the epitome of luxury. Billy Hart's photography shop has moved into the former post office, but the pillar-box remains.

A slightly later view of the same scene. The Clifton premises are now occupied by Woodwards Toy Store, but this would later become Lye Market. The shops on the left, opposite, fell victim to the massive redevelopment from the 1960s on. Hughes' shop was once occupied by the well-known Lye butcher Pharoah Adams, and the typewriter shop was once Laura Foxall's shoe shop.

The area once known as Lye Village. In the centre is the Unitarian church, which enjoyed two major phases of building. The original was erected through the good works of the Rev. James Scott of Netherend in 1806. The tower and extensions were added in 1861. The clock commemorated Mr Scott's achievements, but was replaced by an illuminated model to celebrate the Queen's coronation in 1953. The shops on the left, including Sankeys secondhand shop, succumbed to the redevelopment as did the Dock behind them.

The High Street beyond the Unitarian church, early 1960s. The public house is the Lord Dudley Arms. It, together with other buildings around, was demolished for redevelopment.

Chapel Street before redevelopment. At the bottom on the left are the former police station and sleeping quarters for single policemen. On the right is Wilkes' paper shop; previously it had belonged to the Gardeners.

A Bill Pardoe photograph of the junction of Union Street and Chapel Street, before the 1960s redevelopment. There is an air of dereliction about the house in the foreground, but its neighbour is still spick and span. The bricklaying is typical of Lye.

More typical Lye brickwork in the Dock. This was a narrow back street running parallel to the High Street from the end of Talbot Street to Vicarage Road. The church steeple is dimly visible in the centre.

Another Bill Pardoe shot of a long-gone Lye back street. More interesting than its exact location are the buildings. On the left is a mud hut which has been much altered by the addition of a brick skin and dormer window. Judging by its shuttered window, the building on the right was probably a nail or chain shop.

Church Street looking towards the library, early 1960s. The original Salvation Army Citadel is in the left foreground. Below it is the Liberal Club, opened in 1906. At the bottom of the street is the Temperance Hall, erected in 1874 and later used as a cinema. The projectionist's box may be seen jutting out over the pavement.

The Cross Walks near the junction with Church Street. This was before the demolition of the whole area in the 1960s. Note the cobbler's shop, the typical brickwork of the houses and the brick pavement.

A Bill Pardoe photograph recording the devastation of the drastic redevelopment of the 1960s. This is The Waste looking down towards Lye church and Cross Walks. Mount Tabor chapel is on the left. Known as the Top Chapel, it opened in 1872 and closed in 1964. Mrs Obedience (commonly known as 'Badie') Dickens' drapery shop, painted white, had once housed the first Co-operative shop in the Birmingham area. The ornate-fronted building belonged to Stan Bedford, a well-known hawker and one-time frost cog manufacturer.

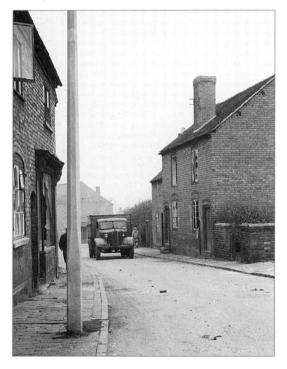

A depressing view of Talbot Street in the run up to redevelopment. The most interesting feature is the use of local bricks, blue engineering ones for the pavement and red ones laid in a 'slap-happy' fashion for the nineteenth-century houses. Welch's bike shop is on the left.

The Waste and Cross Walks. Another Bill Pardoe record of the devastating effect of 1960s redevelopment. The houses and shops of Cross Walks Road and Cross Street have disappeared, including the last surviving mud hut, 33 Cross Walks.

Looking up Belmont Road from the demolished Cross Walks Road. The Top Bell public house and the Unitarian Parsonage are visible on the horizon. The last mud hut in Lye was sited behind the stunted tree beyond the bench.

King Street, 1987. The Princess Royal visited Ben Baker's horse-shoe factory to help celebrate its centenary (see page 83). She is accompanied by Ray Burn, the company chairman. The firm later moved to new premises on the Hayes.

Ludgbridge Brook Road, Lye. The cottages stood at the bottom of Perrins Lane and were probably originally farm labourers' cottages, but in the 1851 census all the tenants were nail-makers. The houses have long disappeared, but were still standing when Springfield Avenue was constructed in 1931.

CHAPTER TWO

BUILDINGS

It is hard to imagine that this is a Black Country scene; however, it is the view from Wollescote House, c. 1912.

Wollescote House, *c.* 1912. This was originally a timber-framed farmhouse adjoining Wollescote Hall, house of the Milward family who purchased the farm in the 1750s to extend their estates. It was leased to various families and in 1912 became the home of Charles Howell and his wife Viola. Charles was a director of Noah Hingley's and Hartshill Iron Company, and Viola was the daughter of John Feeney, arts and music critic of the *Birmingham Post*. The house and its grounds were purchased in 1930 by Ernest Stevens as part of his gift of a park to the people of Lye and Wollescote. The house was demolished in 1965.

The courtyard steps which led up to the garden of Wollescote House, *c.* 1912. The part of the house visible on the right illustrates that it was much older than its façade (shown in the previous photograph) suggests. Note the dog kennel.

Dorothy, daughter of Charles and Viola Howell, admiring the dovecote at Wollescote House, *c.* 1919. Dorothy was an accomplished musician and achieved considerable fame as a composer (see also page 122). Born in Handsworth in 1898, she entered the London Royal Academy of Music in 1914 to study piano and composition. In 1919 her orchestral work *Lamia* was played at the Proms, organised by Sir Henry Wood, and rapturously received by audiences and critics alike. In 1924 she was appointed Professor of Harmony and Composition at the Royal Academy of Music, retiring in 1970. She died in 1982. Her music is currently undergoing a revival.

Wesley Perrins posing outside the eighteenth-century nail warehouse (later Foxall's factory) and nailmaster's house at Careless Green, Wollescote. They once belonged to Thomas Perrins, who established the first factory in Lye in 1770. Wesley Perrins was a local councillor, Trades Union leader and Labour MP. Born in 1905, he died in January 1990.

Whitehouse's premises, 63 Stourbridge Road, Hay Green, c. 1900. Mr Whitehouse had a plumbing and decorating business. His daughter married Enoch Boaler (see page 86) who carried on his galvanising and hollow-ware business there. The house has long gone.

John Lavender, fishmonger, stands proudly outside his shop at 210 High Street, Lye, 1911. He was then 47 years old. He was a great animal lover and his horse Bobby, who collected boxes of fresh fish from Lye station most days and also pulled the family trap for weekend country jaunts, was given a day of rest each week. John died in 1923.

John Lavender in his early 20s, in a studio portrait of about 1885.

Emily Jane Lavender, widow of John Lavender, standing outside her shop in Lye High Street in 1935. Before his death John, Emily and their children, Cecil and Kathleen, lived above the shop. With Emily in this photograph are her daughter-in-law and grand-daughter Maureen.

George Bromley's household supplies shop in Lye High Street, *c.* 1890. He is pictured here with his wife Fanny, whom he married in 1883. The premises still stand in 1999 but may disappear with redevelopment of the area. During the war the upper rooms were occupied by the Rose family, evacuated from the Birmingham bombing.

J.T. Worton's Ladies' Department, early 1920s. Worton's was a large draper's shop in the High Street next to the Congregational church. Featured in the photograph are, centre back, manageress Annie Taylor, Annie Hemming on her left, and to her right is Lily Burford. Gladys Clewitt is front right and on the left is Connie Stevens. The girl in the centre is unnamed.

Mrs Chance and her son Glen, 1920. She had a grocery shop on the Cross Walks, opposite no. 33. Clarence Chance, the Lye church organist, was her elder son.

No. 33 Cross Walks, the last well-known mud hut in Lye. Such houses were built on the Lye Waste area in large numbers from the late seventeenth century on, using local clay. Originally they were thatched, but by the time of its demolition in the early 1960s no. 33 had an asbestos-tiled roof and its walls were faced with cement.

Mrs Edith Heathcote with grand-daughters Sheila and Pam behind her house in Hickman Street, Stambermill, early 1950s. She was renowned locally for her delicious cakes and groaty pudding. Her house is built of local bricks with the typical heavy mortaring. The dolly maiden hanging on the wall was the precursor of the modern washing machine!

Broadfields. This was the house and surgery in Stourbridge Road (and opposite Engine Lane) built in 1901 by Dr H.C. Darby (1869–1937). The doctor was a popular man and a good doctor (see page 115). Before the First World War he pioneered the training of nurses and ambulancemen in the stopping of haemorrhage. In 1894 he became Medical Officer of Health to the newly formed Lye and Wollescote UDC. The house still stands.

Layland Brothers' Garage, Hayes Lane, shortly after its opening in 1951. It was started by brothers Frank and Basil, who had previously had a motor repair business in Vicarage Road.

Layland Brothers' Garage, 1970s. It is obviously now a thriving business. By the 1990s it had more than doubled in size. The brothers are old car enthusiasts and regularly appear at motoring events in their immaculate vehicles.

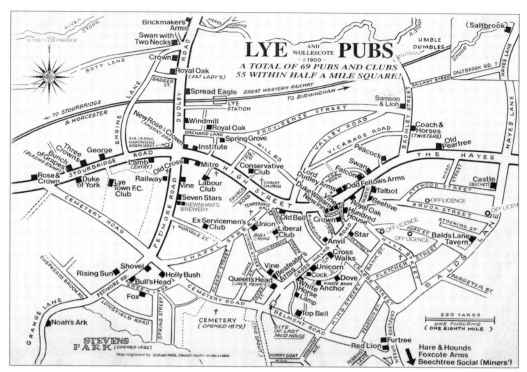

A map marking the location of the many pubs for which Lye was renowned in earlier days. It was researched and drawn by well-known local cartoonist Len Pardoe, whose business premises were the Old Pear Tree pub on the Hayes.

The Coach and Horses Inn, Bromley Street, c. 1911. It was kept by the Taylor family and several members are in the picture. Top left is Harold Taylor; top right is brother Stan. In the doorway is Lilias Taylor flanked (left to right) by her other children, Laura, Billy, Vernon and Priscilla. She moved in in 1911 and left when she was 81, dying at the age of 93.

The Coach and Horses, *c.* 1911. Note that several improvements have been made since the Taylors moved in. The licensee, Samuel Taylor, is standing beside the horse. The driver is Benjamin Taylor (no relation), who lived next door. His wife Charlotte stands in the doorway.

A Sunday get-together at the rear of the Coach and Horses, *c.* 1912. Priscilla Taylor is at back left, and smoking a pipe at the other end of the row is her father Samuel. At the front extreme left is Laura, then Stan, Billy sitting on someone's knee and centre front baby Vernon. Note the ubiquitous mangle behind Laura, and that all the men are wearing a flower in their buttonhole.

The Hundred House pub in Skeldings Lane. The area around it was once known as Slack Mound. Note the old gas street lamp lying on the ground; perhaps the boy surveying it is mourning the end of the joy of swinging from it on a rope. The new lamp signals the end of an era; soon, in the 1960s, the whole area would be bulldozed.

The Hundred House decorated to celebrate VE Day in May 1945. It was kept by Frank and Florence Pardoe, who brewed beer on the premises.

The White Horse public house on Cross Walks. The redevelopment of the Waste and Cross Walks has already begun, as new houses are being erected to the right, beyond Pope Street.

'Polly Brooks's' Lye Cross Inn, *c.* 1920. Lye Cross was an important road junction as far back as Saxon times and there would have been a hostelry on the site for centuries. Male customers pose for the camera before embarking on a trip. Third left on the front row is Henry Skidmore, recently returned from service on the front in the First World War.

An atmospheric shot of the Old Bell Inn in the snow, 1960s. It is snugly wedged between the old bank on the right and Collins' green-grocery on the left. Mr Albert Collins also ran a coach company offering day trips to the seaside and other delights. This is a Billy Hart postcard, one of a collection available at Hart's Photography in the High Street.

The Anvil, Cross Walks, 1960s. The name commemorates the old Lye industries of anvil-making and the manufacture of nails, which used an anvil.

The Old Red Lion, Careless Green, Wollescote, *c.* 1900. Licensee James Elcock stands in the doorway with helpe
Emma Herrin to the right. Mrs Elcock poses at an upstairs window.

Interior of the new Red Lion, Careless Green, early 1950s. It replaced the building shown above between the war
This is a photograph of Lye and Wollescote Allotment Association's Harvest Festival. Bill Willetts is on the rigl
and his father, the club secretary, on the left.

CHAPTER THREE

CHAPELS & CHURCHES

St Mark's Church, Stambermill, and its hall, 1960s. The church was opened by Lord Lyttelton in 1870 and the hall in 1914. Both were demolished as part of the redevelopment scheme.

The Rev. A.G. Lewis, Vicar of Stambermill. He is photographed in his study at the vicarage in Cemetery Road in 1922. A bachelor, he was a popular incumbent who served his parish faithfully for nearly forty years.

The wedding of Fred Burford and Ethel Johnson, which took place at St Mark's in 1928. Fred worked for Worton's the tailor in Lye High Street; his father-in-law Mr Johnson, on the right, was a cobbler on Lye Waste near the Falcon Inn. Ethel's sister Alice was bridesmaid.

St Mark's football team, 1901. Most churches and chapels sported their own football teams at the turn of the century, a successful way of recruiting young members. Unfortunately no names are available. Note the smart kit and the popularity of pipe-smoking.

St Mark's football team, 1914. Second left in the back row is Edwin Morris, son of the local jeweller, who was destined to become Archbishop of Wales; fourth left in the front is Tim Cartwright, son of Elisha Cartwright of Centre Building fame.

Christ Church, Lye, after the spire was added in 1885 and before the war memorial was erected in 1926. The church was built through the good offices of local industrialist Thomas Hill in 1813, using bricks made on site.

The interior of Lye church in the 1960s, before its modernisation. Many of the stained glass windows were made by Bill Pardoe who lived in the family home opposite, where his father had a photographic business.

Christ Church, Lye, after the erection of the war memorial and before the removal of the spire in the 1980s.

Above: Lye church choir, 1948. Back row, left to right: Bill Smith, Mr Bashford snr, Mr Abel, Mr Cox, Clarence Chance (organist), Eber Wooldridge, Dennis Hart, Claude Holt, Derek Allcock, George Clews, Geoffrey Westwood. Middle row: Server, -?-, Mary Hill, Phyllis Bottomley, Phyllis Clews, Enid Knowles, Janet Scott, John Wooldridge, ? Bashford. Front row: Trevor Smith, Terry Hart, Rev. Frederick Vickery Rev. Mr Stuart-King, Vicar of Lye 1920–30, John Smith, Peter Fradgley.

Lye church outing to Malvern, c. 1930. Back row, left to right: Len Bashford, Cliff Taylor. Front row: Madge Round, Clarence Chance, Elsie Whitehouse.

Lye church outing to Stourport, June 1926. The Rev. Stuart King and his wife, with Mr T. Hodgkiss, Churchwarden, to the right are surrounded by a multitude of church members, including a very young baby with its mother, May Meredith.

Lye church members camping at Arley, ?late 1920s. Seated around the table are, left to right, Clarence Chance, John Forest, Percy Wooldridge, Cliff Taylor, Len Bashford, Ann Brettell, May Norris, Mary Bradley, Maggie Chance and Elsie Whitehouse.

The Unitarian church was known as the village church, and when built in 1806 by the Rev. James Scott it had a great civilising influence on the lawless inhabitants of Lye Waste. It was substantially rebuilt in his memory in 1861, but by the time of this photograph taken in the mid-'70s it is showing signs of decay; the pinnacle of the clock tower has gone. The last service was held on 21 July 1991 and the premises were sold for secular use.

The Christadelphian church in Pedmore Road. At its side is Morvale Street. It was built in 1932 and is still operating as a church in 1999.

The former Lye Salvation Army citadel in Church Street, *c.* 1965. The Army came to Lye in 1881 and was an immediate success. The citadel was built in about 1900.

The Salvation Army band playing in Summer Street on a fine summer's day, mid-1960s. An audience of small boys is enjoying the sunshine.

The opening of Hodge Hill chapel, Wollescote, 10 September 1938. The tall young man on the left is Wesley Perrins and next but one to him are Frank Lowe and Arthur Bourne. The minister, the Rev. Mr Calloway, stands behind the gentleman with the buttonhole on the right. Harry Head and Noah Jeavons are on the left of the minister and the lady on the right is Laura Foxall, High Street shoe shop owner. The photograph was taken by a well-known Lye figure, W.E.G. Smith.

Hayes Lane Methodist chapel was built in 1896 and closed in May 1975, when the trustees felt it was no longer practical to open for worship. They decided that the proceeds of its sale should be used towards a new church in Lye. This photograph was taken in the mid-1960s.

Mount Tabor or Top Chapel, on Cross Walks. It was opened in 1872 and closed in 1964. It was later demolished as part of the redevelopment scheme.

The cemetery chapels. At the time of the opening of Lye and Wollescote cemetery in 1878 there were great divisions between Anglicans and Non-conformists which did not end with death, and the graveyard was divided. The chapel on the left and that half of the cemetery were for Anglicans, while the right-hand side was for Non-conformists.

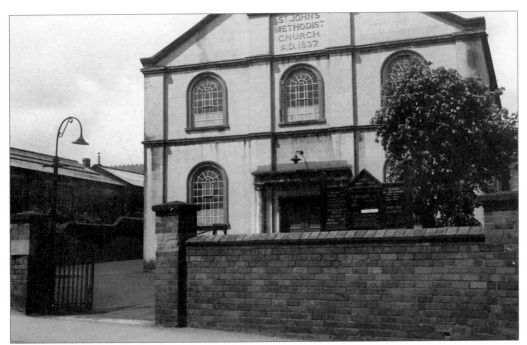

St John's Methodist church in Chapel Street, formerly Dark Lane. Built on the site of an earlier chapel in 1837, it closed in 1968 and was later demolished.

The fine interior of St John's Methodist church. Note the clock partially visible at the back, which preachers could use to keep an eye on the time.

1939 ✝ 1945
IN HONOURED MEMORY OF
RONALD PRICE AND SIDNEY HART
SCHOLARS OF THE SUNDAY SCHOOL
WHO GAVE THEIR LIVES FOR OUR FREEDOM.
MAY WE BE WORTHY OF THEIR SACRIFICE.

A poignant memorial formerly in St John's church. It commemorates two church members who died on active service within four days of each other. Sidney Hart was a Royal Marine who was killed evacuating troops from Dunkirk, and Ron Price a naval stoker.

Ronald Price died when his ship, HMS *Kite*, was torpedoed on the North Atlantic Convoy run to Russia. It sank with all hands. Here he is photographed in his naval uniform shortly before his death.

A memorial to Joseph Attwood and his wife Mary in St John's Methodist church. Joseph was a member of the Birmingham banking and Chartist family. He owned a vice and anvil forge on the Hayes.

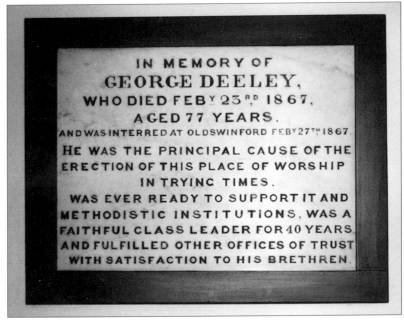

A memorial to George Deeley. He was born when Lye was in turmoil and lawlessness and ungodliness widespread. It was the influence of church and chapel which eventually 'civilised' the community.

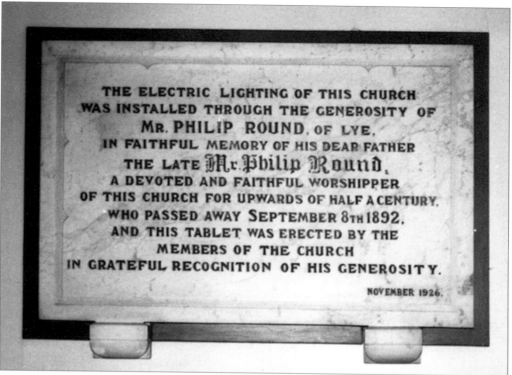

THE ELECTRIC LIGHTING OF THIS CHURCH
WAS INSTALLED THROUGH THE GENEROSITY OF
MR. PHILIP ROUND, OF LYE,
IN FAITHFUL MEMORY OF HIS DEAR FATHER
THE LATE Mr. Philip Round,
A DEVOTED AND FAITHFUL WORSHIPPER
OF THIS CHURCH FOR UPWARDS OF HALF A CENTURY,
WHO PASSED AWAY SEPTEMBER 8TH 1892,
AND THIS TABLET WAS ERECTED BY THE
MEMBERS OF THE CHURCH
IN GRATEFUL RECOGNITION OF HIS GENEROSITY.
NOVEMBER 1926.

A practical memorial to a faithful worshipper at St John's. Philip Round's son installed electric lighting in the church in his father's memory. The Rounds owned a hollow-ware factory in Orchard Lane (see page 87).

The Primitive Methodist church Sunday school in Connop's Lane. The chapel was built in 1831, but was made unsafe when, during demolition of the outdated Sunday School premises for rebuilding, the gable end of the church collapsed in July 1974.

Above: A 'Prims' wedding. The wedding of Donald
Richards, a well-known local church organist, and Freda
Wassell, took place at the Primitive Methodist church on
31 January 1948. Back row, left to right: Mrs Martha
Wassell, Rev. Forrester, George Wassell, Alfred Richards,
best man Joe Taylor. Front row: Sandra Willets, bride and
groom, Mrs Elsie Richards and bridegroom's grandmother,
Ellen Richards.

The Primitive Methodist chapel forms the background for
this snapshot, 1945. The children are, left to right, Geoffrey
Millward, Kenneth Harris and Patricia Harris.

CHAPTER FOUR

CHILDHOOD

The children of Charles and Viola Howell outside Wollescote House, c. 1912. Back row, left to right: Alfred, Mary, Carlo (killed in action, 1917) and Winnie. Front row: Dorothy and Clifford. The dog is Colin.

Fishmonger John Lavender and his wife Emily Jane. They are pictured with their baby son, Cecil, in 1893. Cecil became a well-known musician and conductor when he grew up.

Lavender family group, 1902. By the time of this portrait the Lavenders had a daughter, Kathy. The picture was taken by William Pardoe of Vicarage Road, a well-known Lye photographer who passed on his talent to his son, Bill.

Kathy Lavender and aunt, Hetty Watson, her mother's sister, 1911. Note the popularity of *broderie anglaise* in female fashions.

A pensive Kathleen Lavender aged 17,
1917. Her brother was then a POW in
Germany, so perhaps this explains her sad
expression.

Mr and Mrs Price with daughter Gladys.
They were captured on film when Mr Price
was home on leave from war service. Gladys
was Carnival Queen in 1930 and was
crowned by Sir Cedric Hardwicke, the
Hollywood film star (see pages 112, 113
and 114). Their son Ronald was killed on
active service in the Second World War
(see page 53).

Bossie and Alfred Perks with their eldest son Ernie, 1926. For a time they were stewards at Hill and Blakemore Liberal Club, but later returned to live in Lye.

Cecil Lavender's first school. He is standing front left. The boy third from the right in the back row is Cedric Hardwicke, son of the local doctor. The photograph was taken at Mr W. Pardoe's studio in Vicarage Road in 1897. The school was probably the small private establishment opposite Lye Cross House, the Hardwicke residence. It was run in an upper room of the post office by Mrs Freeman, the postmistress, and her two daughters.

Lye National School, on the corner of the High Street and Vicarage Road, was opened on 10 May 1840, Queen Victoria's 21st birthday. It was a charity school provided by the Church of England which used the monitorial system of instruction to keep down costs. The premises later became the Church Hall when a new school was built behind it. The site is now occupied by the Salvation Army citadel.

Lye Church School infants class, 1921. The little girl on the extreme right of the third row is Violet Harper. Born on 5 March 1916, she died tragically in 1923 when a vaccination went wrong.

rchard Lane School opened in 1882, complying with the 1870 Education Act which made education mpulsory for all children whatever their means. The new school had mixed infants', boys' and girls' epartments and was administered by a locally elected voluntary School Board, being financed by local rates. oday only the caretaker's house on the right remains.

treasured photograph of a carnival group, 1920s. It is assembled in Orchard Lane School playground. The embers are older schoolchildren and the girls are dressed as flowers. The girl standing on the extreme left is ouisa Wood who sadly died a few years later in childbirth leaving a young family.

Stambermill School group, 1926. The school was a church foundation for 'mixed' infants and juniors when it was built in 1852. The premises were enlarged in 1894. The building still exists but has now been converted to industrial use.

A class at Wollescote Infants School, 1928. The little girls wear aprons and many in the front row wear boots.

Wollescote Infants School opened, as a consequence of the 1870 Education Act, in 1897, the year of Queen Victoria's Diamond Jubilee, and unlike all the other Lye and Wollescote schools existing then is still going strong.

Wollescote Primary School swimming pool under construction, 1974. It was built with funds raised by the school and subsidised by the local council. Constructed with the assistance of parents and teachers, it opened on 2 March 1975. Some of those involved are pictured here. Top: Dennis Tibbetts and Roy Bennett. Standing, left to right: Jim Broad, Geoff Attwood, Mick Lees, -?-, Geoff Smith, and Dick Nordon is in the foreground. Up the ladder is Headmaster William Whitworth, who passed away in 1999.

Wollescote Primary School athletics team, 1981. Pictured, amongst others, are Jackie Bridgewater, Amand Kendrick, Paula Cox, Lisa Barrett, Jason Wakeman, Dean Yates (Captain), Jason Tomlinson, Dean Hill, Abid Alta Glynn Taylor, Craig Lees, Mohammed Mahmood, Jamie Morris and Darren Hickman. The boys' team wa Stourbridge Schools AA Champion that year, beating their old rivals Wollaston into second place.

Cemetery Road Infants School group, c. 1926. In true Lye tradition of giving everyone and everything a nicknam this was always known as 'the little school'. Built in 1882, it closed down several years ago, although th buildings still exist. Second from the right on the front row is Norman Clewes. It is impossible not to notice th change in appearance and demeanour of the schoolchildren illustrated in these two photographs.

A dancing class at Crabbe Street Girls School, *c.* 1918–20. It is interesting to see such an activity at a time when the curriculum was rigid and mainly devoted to maths, English and RE. The enlightened approach to education is mirrored in the light paintwork, potted plants and pictures.

The rear of Valley Road School. It was built in 1911 to provide secondary education to older children previously attending Orchard Lane School, as a result of pressure from the Rev. Mr Wrigley, the Unitarian minister, a Worcestershire County Councillor. Only the domestic science block stands today, and is in industrial use.

The cast of Valley Road Secondary Modern School's pantomime, 1948. It was performed by girls from the third year, and was entitled 'Beauty and the Beast'. Back row, left to right: Jean Southall, Lilian Evans, Iris Porter, Shirley Taylor, Doreen Leggett, Kathleen Taylor, Norma Brooks and Lavinia Wall. Front row: Winifred Checketts, Dorothy Cartwright and Beryl Lees.

Mrs Deeley's sewing class, Valley Road School, 26 July 1948. The girls are modelling outfits they made that year and they all look a credit to their teacher. Back row, left to right: Sylvia Davies, Mavis Jones, June Cook, Winifred Checketts, Connie Loveridge, Margaret Shaw, Iris Porter and Doris Merrick. Front row: Betty McTighe, Audrey Jones, Jean Southall, Dorreen Leggett and Shirley Taylor.

Frederick Hill became Headmaster of Lye Church Boys School at a very early age and died on 1 January 1918. There is a stained glass window in his memory in Christ Church, Lye.

Harold and Stan Taylor, c. 1912. They were the sons of Samuel and Lilias Taylor, licensees of the Coach and Horses in Bromley Street where this photograph was taken. This photograph is ideal for students of costume.

Left: Priscilla Taylor. She was a sister of the two brothers on the previous page, photographed outside the Coach and Horses, *c.* 1912. Once again she provides a wealth of information to students of costume.

Below: Priscilla's music examination results, 1918. It is a pity that she sat the examination on 11 November 1918 and gained 100 per cent, for the family often wondered whether the examiners were elated by the news of the cessation of hostilities in the First World War. They had no need to worry, for Priscilla went on to become a noted piano teacher.

A young J. Vernon Kendrick, aged 16, 1922.
He was apprenticed to his uncle, the local
undertaker, on leaving school and took over
the business when his uncle died.

A young Lydia Perks, *c.* 1915. Her parents
lived in Vicarage Road, the street where
W. Pardoe had his photographic studio, so
this picture would have been taken there.
Note the pretty dress and hair bows.

Arthur Boaler as a toddler. He was born in 1905, the son of Enoch Boaler, hollow-ware manufacturer in Stourbridge Road. He wears a very fashionable sailor suit. Arthur married Lydia Perks and carried on the family business all his working life.

Arthur Boaler in his early teens, c. 1920. The photograph is another good example of changing fashions. At that time men's caps were extremely large and boots were widely worn. This is a studio portrait taken by W. Pardoe.

CHAPTER FIVE

WORK

A Bill Pardoe stained glass window in Lye church. It depicts the church surrounded by the factories and industries of the town. In the foreground may be seen a shovel, bucket, anvil and hammer.

The Lees family, *c.* 1900. In spite of the early industrialisation of Lye there were still several farms in the area, and the Lees were prominent in the farming community. Esther had five daughters – Eliza, Esther Ann, Fanny, Annie Louisa and Elsie who died in infancy, and six sons. The sons were, standing, left to right, William James, Frank Edward Charles, and Thomas; seated, David and George. Esther and her sons ran Lees Bros Dairy in Dudley Road. After her death in 1911 her son William and grandson William Taylor expanded the business to include Foxcote House Farm, and as Lees and Taylor delivered milk locally by horse and cart. David and Edward went on to run their own farms, Banks Farm and Pedmore Hall Farm.

Stan Taylor, *c.* 1914. He helped out at Yardley's Farm delivering milk. Manpower would have been short at this time, because of conscription during the First World War and the wholesale slaughter of British soldiers.

Ventilation mine shaft. This is the last vestige of the coal industry in Lye. It stands in Colemans, by tradition where the Huguenots first made glass in the area, on the edge of that coal seam which helped give the Black Country its name.

The Brickmaker's Arms, 1960s. The presence of clay and fireclay encouraged the growth of the brick industry in all three communities covered by this book. A reminder of this is the name of the pub, since demolished. In 1866 it was used as a coroner's court when Mr Lees committed suicide in the hayloft of Dudley Road Farm. It was thought he killed himself because his best milking cow died at a time of agricultural depression.

Bagley's Mill sluice. Industry came early to Lye because of the wealth of raw materials – coal, clay, lime, sand and ironstone – and the power of the River Stour. There were many forges along the river and its tributaries. Bagley's Mill is marked on a map of 1699, and is on the site of a Saxon ford.

Nineteenth-century nailer's block. This was used by Wesley Perrins' mother in the 1880s to make nails; it is a stone anvil and would have been used in a backyard workshop.

An unusual Christmas card: it hardly inspires the festive spirit. Mrs Brettell looks undernourished and poorly clad in her 'hurden' apron. The girl peeping shyly round the door is Alice Pearson, who became a lifelong Socialist and champion of the workers in the sweated industries of nail and chain-making. She was a friend of Jennie Lee, wife of Aneurin Bevan, founder of the National Health Service. Mrs Brettell is making handles for pans and buckets.

The roof apex of Perrins' Chain Works, Careless Green. This photograph illustrates two points: it gives the date of the founding of the firm, and provides evidence of the excellence of the products of the local brickyards.

Above: Mr H.T. Hazelwood (1847–1934), frost cog manufacturer. He was apprenticed to Phileman Taylor, his brother-in-law, in his nail shop on Waste Bank, but in 1882 established his own business in Crabbe Street. He manufactured different types of frost cogs and frost screws.

Below: Examples of hand-made products. They were made by such firms as Baker's, Hazelwood's, Turner's, and Perry and Brookes'. Columns 1 and 2: anti-slip horse-shoe nails; column 3: frost screws, which were superior to the nails as they kept the shoe on and were anti-slip; column 4 top: frost cogs, which were slipped into a hole specially punched into the horse-shoe; centre: known as the Caledonian toe-piece because it was made for the Scottish market; bottom two: these have blunt heads to fill the holes until bad weather necessitated the use of the genuine frost cog.

The ruler is worthy of mention. Its maker, Helix, was founded in 1887 and until 1955 was based at factories in Balsall Heath and Oldbury. In 1955 it moved to larger premises in Engine Lane, Lye, and completely overhauled its marketing practices to deal directly with retailers. The owner's widow, Elsie Lawson, further expanded the overseas market in the 1960s. Today it is a world-famous thriving business manufacturing hundreds of items of educational equipment.

Benjamin Baker advertisement in the *Farriers Journal*, July 1937. The top right-hand corner shows the original workshop in King Street in 1887 and the large drawing shows the premises in 1937. In 1993 the firm moved to new quarters at the Hayes, giving an extra 50 per cent workspace.

B. Timmins bending horse-shoes at Benjamin Baker's, 1971. The firm made 800 different patterns of horse-shoes and still produces almost that number, exporting worldwide particularly to the USA, Canada and Middle and Far East.

Derek Griffiths, managing director (now retired) of Ben Baker's. He is inspecting horse-shoes in the King Street premises. It is now the only firm worldwide producing hand-made horse-shoes.

Baker's advertisement, *Farriers Journal*, September 1956. The cost of the entry was £5 10s. The illustration of farming practice is a far cry from modern procedures, and is a charming piece of nostalgia.

								Voucher No.
Cash to Bought Ledger	Carriage	Travelling Expenses	Sundry Purchases	Trade Expenses	Printing and Stationery	Postage and Telegrams		
ne 21	A Cartwright	D Timmins	J Taylor	Simkiss				
ne 22	B H Baker	Pearson	A Spittle					
ne 23	J Phillips	Wooldridge	Burgess					
June 24	L Smith	Brettle	Welsh	Simkiss				
ne 25	J Hatton	Weston	S Hatton	Perry				
ne 26	S Handy	A Hill	R Handy					
ne 27	W Pardoe	R Handy	Collins	Taylor				
ne 28	Sidway	E Timmins	Burgess	H Perry				
June 29	Chas Smith	A Pardoe	J Baker	C Smith				
Jan 30	Sim Baker	W Hatton						
July 1	San Phillips	J Bashford	B Baker	Timmins				
July 2	D Timmins	J Smith	Pitchford					
July 3	A Cartwright	J Taylor	W Cartwright					
July 4	B H Baker	Pearson	Spittle A					
ly 5	J Phillips	Burgess	Wooldridge					
aly 6	L Smith	Welsh						
July 7	J Hatton	Weston	Perry					
July 8	S Handy	Davis	A Hill	R Handy				
July 9	W Pardoe	R Handy	Collins	Taylor				
July 10	Sidway	Burgess	Perry					
July 11	C Smith	A Pardoe	Chas Smith					
July 12	L Cook	S Baker						
July 13	S Phillips	F Bashford	Timmins					
July 14	D Smith	D Timmins	Pitchford					
July 15	A Cartwright	W Cartwright	J Taylor					
July 16	B H Baker	Pearson	A Spittle					
July 17	J Phillips	Wooldridge	Burgess					
July 18	L Smith	Brettle	Welsh	Simkiss				

Fire watching duty rota, Ben Baker's: a page from the firewatching book for parts of June and July 1941. The men were paid 3s per night from Monday to Friday and 4s 6d at weekends. The money was paid by the management who were reimbursed by the local Council. The firewatchers would report for work the morning after their duty.

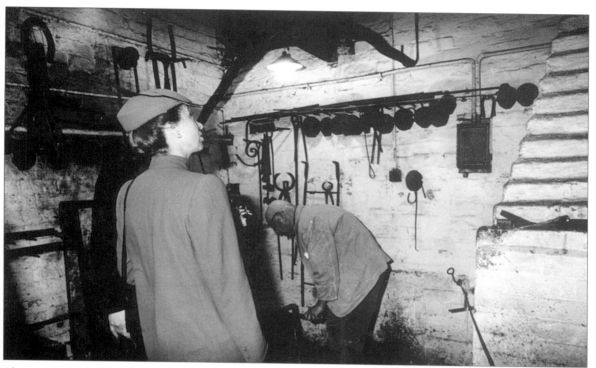

Above: A royal visitor. Princess Anne, a customer and accomplished horsewoman who represented England at the Olympic Games, tours the King Street premises of Benjamin Baker. Here she is in the toolroom with Charlie Smith. The Princess Royal visited the firm as part of its centenary celebrations.

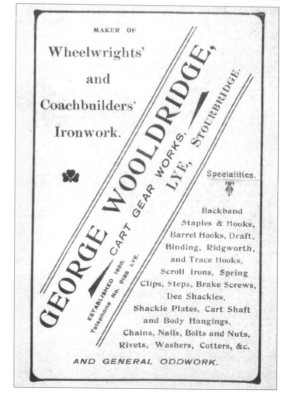

Right: A turn-of-the-century advertisement for George Wooldridge of Balds Lane. The firm specialised in ironwork accessories for horse-drawn vehicles when first founded.

Gary Newey making a small metal casting at Wooldridge's, 1970s.

Wooldridge's workforce, 1970s. Harold Heathcote is on the extreme left, with fellow workers Mervyn Griffin, Bob Dunn, Ken Willetts, Desmond Willetts (wearing gloves), Ian ? and Charlie Hart.

Making screws at John Perks', Church Street. These were used on lorries where the body was tipped by a cranked handle operated by the driver.

Drop stamper at 'Johnty' Perks', 1960s. The firm was founded in 1861 as a nail-making concern but it later specialised in springs – first for horse-drawn vehicles and then for lorries.

Enoch Boaler (1874–1933). He carried on a galvanising and enamelling business at the rear of the family home in Stourbridge Road. A quiet man, he was nevertheless very interested in and supportive of local affairs. In the First World War he was a Special Constable.

Boaler workforce, 1920s. On the left is Arthur Boaler who eventually took over the business, and the young girl is his sister Vera. Billy Bridgewater is on the extreme right.

Philip Round's factory, Orchard Lane. It was established in 1849 for the manufacture of nails, chains and vices. In 1874 it began to produce hollow-ware goods.

J. & P. Round trade stand at Stockport Show, 1928. Philip is shown with his secretary Gladys Underwood, and with a wide display of goods which the firm manufactured.

Edging and flanging machine. This was made in Lye exclusively for the bucket trade. It was one of a line of five machines which produced a bucket from a blanked outside to a 'head', ready for ears, handle and hoop.

Before power presses came into their own and even in recent times (for short runs) bench shears were used to cut out sheet metal parts. They were made in Lye by specialist blacksmiths.

The former Hingley and Lamb factory. This firm's premises were in Railway Street, now renamed Stourvale Road. It produced hollow-ware goods. Several years ago it closed down because of the decline in trade and the premises were taken over. However, the name of the original owners can still be seen on the pediment. During the war the firm went over to essential war work and the men worked extended hours, requiring the delivery of both dinner and tea. Children delivering these to the workforce were paid the handsome sum of 2d per week.

Higgins Press at Churchill Forge, near Kidderminster. This press was purchased secondhand from the makers, Higgins and Sons, Regency Works, Lye, by Benjamin Bache in 1925. It was used in the production of industrial ladles using water power. The forge is now an educational trust and is occasionally open to the public. Though the press ceased to work commercially in the late 1960s, it is hoped to use it in ladle-making demonstrations on open days in the future.

The staff of Cook's, Star Street, *c.* 1953. This small firm manufactured wheelbarrows, garden rollers and machine guards. On the left of the group is Harold Heathcote; in the centre stands Fred Cartwright, and the dark-haired girl beside Fred is Lily Blunt.

Cook's, Star Street, *c.* 1953. Harold Heathcote poses beside some of the products made by the firm.

Frank Wade's, Timmis Road, Stambermill, *c.* 1962. This factory produced ploughshares, and here the girls are examining finished ones to check that there were no mistakes during manufacture. Joan Heathcote is on the right and Betty Wood, brandishing a hammer, stands behind her. Note the old Lye tradition of wearing 'hurden' aprons, often made from old sacks.

Perry and Brookes', Cemetery Road, *c.* 1970. The firm made nuts and bolts and other ironmongery. Although it has ceased trading, the premises are still used industrially. Fashion-conscious Sheila Heathcote takes a break from work to pose for the camera.

Bantock's horses, 1928. The Bantock family originated in Scotland, but Thomas Bantock moved to Wolverhampton in 1849 and nine years later was building wagons for the GWR. His son Albert made a fortune as road and canal haulage contractor for the railway. In Lye the horses collected goods from the local factories and delivered them to the railway goods yard at the station. In this photograph they are part of the parade at the carnival.

Waiting for the hoppin' train, Lye station, c. 1950. Often the only holiday Lye folk had was hop-picking in the Worcestershire and Herefordshire countryside in the autumn. In reality it was no holiday, but they were out in the fresh air and ate well. Some hop-pickers were taken by lorry to the hop yards; the picking-up point was behind the Clifton cinema.

CHAPTER SIX

LEISURE

*The illicit motor-bike, c. 1907. Cecil Lavender bought himself a motor-cycle without his parents'
knowledge before he was sixteen. He bought it in order to ride to Kinver Edge
to meet a young lady.*

Above: Lye and Wollescote Allotment Association, 1953. Secretary Billy Willetts stands in the centre of the front row while his father is on the extreme right. George Billingham is behind Billy on the left and Arnold Eveson is behind Billy on the right. The photograph was taken at the annual potato competition and Mr Joyner, the Parks Superintendent, who checked the weights is on the extreme left.

LYE & WOLLESCOTE ALLOTMENT ASSOCIATION
— President: Ald.G.A.COOK. —

RESULTS OF 1953 POTATO COMPETITION

1.	W.B.Willetts	181 lbs.		
2.	J.Raybould	174 "	7	ozs.
3.	A.Eveson	169 "	4	"
4.	J.Willetts	140 "	6	"
5.	H.Allen Jnr.	128 "	4	"
6.	J.T.Taylor	126 "	4	"
7.	H.Allen Snr.	118 "	15	"
8.	J.Matthews	105 "	4	"
9.	G.W.Davies	98 "	12	"
10.	G.H.Billingham	97 "	14	"
11.	F.E.Brown	89 "	3	"
12.	L.Wood	81 "	7	"
13.	B.Dunn	76 "	10	"
14.	F.Taylor	62 "	9	"

HEAVIEST ROOT: 40 lbs.14 ozs.
HEAVIEST SINGLE
     POTATO: 3 lbs. 1 oz.

     grown by J.Raybould

Official Checkers:

Mr.R.V.C.Joyner (Park Superintendent).
Mr.Stacey (Head Gardener).

Left: Results of the potato competition, 1953. This is the official card recording the weight of the winning entries.

Lye and Wollescote Allotment Association, *c.* 1953. This is the prize-giving of the potato competition, at which Eric Moody and his sister Miss Eileen Moody, prominent Stourbridge businessfolk, present the prizes. (They were the owners of Mark and Moody's in the High Street.) They are third and fifth from the right on the back row, and Mr Joyner stands between them. Park-keeper Percy Norris, wearing his official cap, is third from the left and second left is Bill Willetts. On the front row are Arnold Eveson, in the centre, and Frank Dickens, third from the right.

Lye Liberal Bowling Team, 1950s. This team includes five brothers. Back row, left to right: Archie Hingley, Dennis Turner, Mr Leedham, -?-, Leslie Turner, -?-, Bob(?) Hudson, Arthur Hall. Front row: Fred Fairman, Clarrie Turner, , Turner, ? Hadlington, -?-, Bob Turner. 'They were always a good team, couldn't lose' was a comment by someone who knew them.

Winners of West Midlands Conservative Bowling League, 1936–38. Back row, left to right: G.H. Harris (secretary), J. Checketts, F. Davies (vice-captain), J. Forest, F. Connop, J. Boaler, B. Taylor, H. Abel, L. Lloyd. Second row: H.E. Hill, J. Davies, J. Stevens (captain), C. Thomas, H. Thompson (treasurer). Front row: L. Kendrick, D. Lloyd (scorer).

Boys' Brigade at camp, 1932. These are members of the 1st Lye Company. Back row, left to right: N. Cookson, F. Johnson, K. Hamblett, J. Wood, D. Watkins. Front row: G. Cartwright and E. Porter (captain).

Boys' Brigade at camp, c. 1935. Back row, left to right: G. Kendrick, D. Brooks, C. Little, S. Hart, J. Beasley, A. Stinton, G.H. Cartwright. Middle row: L. Pearson, L. Cooper. Front row: R. Perks, R. Chapman, R. Foster.

Boys' Brigade at camp, c. 1935. In this photograph the Rev. Taylor Richardson is chatting to members of the Lye 1st Company as he inspects them.

Lye Nursing cadets during the First World War, photographed by William Pardoe. The trio on the left are unnamed. Back row, left to right: ? Wooldridge, -?-, -?-, -?-, -?-, Eliza Hill. Middle row: Rose Poole, Beatt Wassell, Effie Brettell, Hattie Aston, ? Round. Front row: Winnie Bird, Doris Roberts, -?-, -?-, Rita Bellamy.

Lye St John's Ambulance Brigade, *c.* 1920. The local doctor and Medical Officer of Health, Dr Christopher Darby, was a great supporter of the St John's Ambulance Brigade and was Divisional, then County Surgeon for Worcestershire. With such support the Lye branch was always a strong Division, and was the first to have its own permanent headquarters in Worcestershire.

ye Home Guard: a rather indistinct photograph of the Lye Contingent. Denys Brooks is in the centre of the back ow, sporting a cravat. Samuel Hart, on the extreme left of the front row, served in the First World War, and olunteered for active service in the Second. Rejected on health grounds, he then joined the Home Guard. The oys on the front row look too young to be members and are not in uniform, but were no doubt found useful jobs o do.

ye Home Guard: Denys Brooks is on the left of the front row. The two dispatch riders appear to be well equipped or any emergency. However, Denys said that there was little excitement.

Hickman Street Coronation party, 1953. Margaret Parton is third from the right on the front row. She has made a great effort with her costume. Note the blue bricks forming the pavement; these would have been made locally.

Sheila and Pam Heathcote at play, late 1950s. The two little sisters are enjoying themselves in the children's playground adjoining the football and cricket ground at Hay Green.

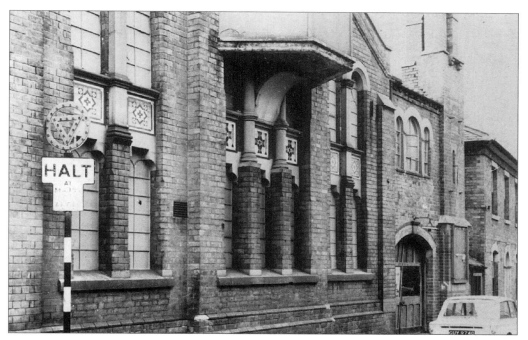

The Temp, 1965. The Temperance Hall was built in 1874 but later became a cinema run by Mr Entwistle, owner of the Danic grocery shop in the High Street. It closed down in the 1960s and was demolished to make way for new houses.

An advertisement for the Clifton, 1937. The Clifton cinema was opened in that year with seating for 1,100 people, over double the capacity of the Temp, which held 460.

Lye 'Scratch' orchestra, *c.* 1908. Cecil Lavender is the young pianist/conductor seated in the centre of the group.

A concert for pensioners held in Lye, 1960s. It was attended by Claude Aston and his wife, Mayor and Mayoress of Stourbridge. He held the office for two terms, 1961–62 and 1967–68.

Pensioners' concert, 1960s.
Another happy snapshot of the
party attended by Claude Aston
and his wife. She was the
daughter of Dr Christopher Darby,
a popular Lye GP.

The cast of *A Midsummer Night's
Dream*, 1926. The curate's wife,
Mrs Herald, produced the play to
raise funds for a new piano for the
church hall. It was performed at
Stourbridge Town Hall for three
nights and raised £120, but the
PCC paid the profits into the
assistant clergy fund to the
consternation of Mrs Herald.
Featured on the back row are, left
to right, -?-, -?-, Maggie Chance,
Hilda Underwood, Emily Hatton,
Winnie Gadd.

Cast of *A Midsummer Night's Dream*, 1926. Back row, left to right: Hilda Underwood, Rita Bellamy. Front row: Evelyn Chance, Hilda Raybould, Katie Jackson, Gladys Underwood.

A Midsummer Night's Dream, 1926. Hilda Underwood poses for the camera in the costume she wore as a fairy. The play was performed again in 1927 as part of the annual Stourbridge Carnival held in aid of Corbett Hospital.

The wedding of Harry and Dorothy Boaler, 1929. The photograph is included here to show the very popular Lye leisure pursuit of pigeon flying: a pigeon loft is in the background of the photograph. Although Lye boasted several pigeon clubs, no material has surfaced on the subject.

Bridesmaids, 1929. This photograph is included for those readers who enjoy wedding photographs. The bridesmaid on the left at Harry's wedding was his future sister-in-law, Lydia Perks. The toddler beside her was his niece Marjorie Stanley.

Wollescote Albion, 1909. The team is assembled outside the Hare and Hounds, Careless Green, December 1909
Licensee Alfred Hodgetts is on the extreme right holding the hand of Newnham Oliver, who grew up to be a well-
known bookmaker. Others pictured are as follows: back row, left to right: W. Phipson (trainer), Ben Stafford, Tom
Kendrick, Tom Roper, William Hart, Fred Allen (secretary). Front row: Elijah Freeman, Jerry Hill, Jepthah
Freeman, Tom Gardener, William Lloyd.

Lye Cricket club in the era of W.G. Grace. Note the variety of headgear and the dashing belts. There
seems to be a shortage of equipment, as the man on the right wears only one pad.

Liberal Club stewards, *c.* 1960. Rose and Clarrie Turner are pictured here behind the bar. Clarrie was one of five brothers who played in the club's invincible bowls team.

Lye Liberal Club members, 1950s. Pictured are, left to right, George Holloway, Percy Clewes and Arthur Wiley. The club premises were built in 1906 in Church Street.

Conservative Club Dance, *c.* 1927. On the front row seventh from the left is Tim Cartwright of Centre Building, seated beside Nancy Harper. On the third row the fourth girl from the left is Bella Eveson née Newnham, a member of the brewery family who lived in Pedmore Road.

Lye Conservative Club, 1930s. Amongst the happy gathering is Mr Ernest Hill, a descendant of the family who were benefactors of Lye in the early nineteenth century. He is on the extreme left. Second from the right is Violet ?, appropriately named for she kept a flower shop in the High Street on the corner of Jackson Street.

Lye Carnival, June 1928. Bill Pardoe was asked by the Mayor, L.J. Cook, to organise this event in Lye to raise money for Corbett Hospital. He may be seen on his AJS motor-cycle in front of the float, preceded by members of the St John's Ambulance Brigade. Note the enormous crowds supporting the event.

Decorated pedestrians, 1928. The girls are assembled in the playground of Orchard Lane School, ready for the grand procession which took place on the Saturday afternoon following a week of other events.

More entrants for the grand procession assemble at Orchard Lane School, 1928.

Even more decorated pedestrians, 1928. Three young ladies were snapped on their way to the procession. The girl on the left is unnamed, Vera Boaler is in the middle and on the right is her future sister-in-law, Lydia Perks.

Apple bobbing competition, 1928. This was one of the events of the carnival organised during the week for local schoolchildren, and the boys are enjoying themselves watched by a large crowd – while local councillors see fair play.

Schoolchildren, Lye Carnival, 1928. On the Wednesday evening of the week-long carnival 3,000 children marched to the Cricket Ground in fancy dress. Bill described it as a moving and colourful occasion, for many of the costumes were made of paper: 'those were the days of poverty before the country had recovered from the disasters of 1914 and unemployment was high'. The weather was fine and here the children are entertaining the large crowd, singing round a piano.

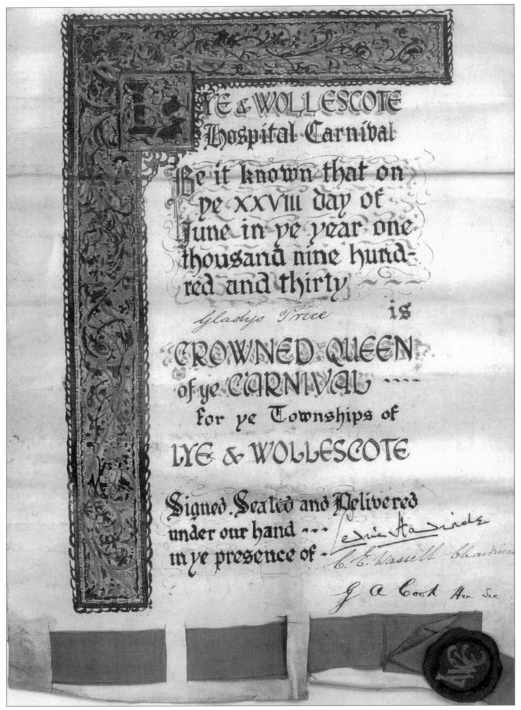

Illuminated Scroll, 1930. As part of the Carnival that year a Beauty Queen was chosen, and this manuscript was presented to the winner, Gladys Price. It was signed by Sir Cedric Hardwicke, who crowned her.

CHAPTER SEVEN

PEOPLE

Lye Carnival Queen, 1930. This snapshot shows Gladys Price on her way to her coronation escorted by her maids of honour, page boys and Stambermill Scouts, to be crowned by locally born Hollywood star Cedric Hardwicke.

Lye Carnival Queen, 1930. This photograph, entered without Gladys' knowledge, was enough to win her the title. She was eighteen years old at the time, but was tragically dead three years later. (She appears as a child on page 60, and her equally tragic brother is featured on page 53.)

Clement Attlee's post-war cabinet, 1945. Lye-born Joseph Westwood, Secretary of State for Scotland, is fourth from the right on the back row. He was born on Lye Waste in 1884, but his father moved to Scotland to find work as a miner. Joseph also worked in the pits but later became political organiser for Scottish colliers, and in 1922 he was elected Labour MP for Peebles; in 1935 he was MP for Stirling and Falkirk. Sadly he and his wife were killed in a motoring accident in 1948.

Lye and Wollescote Councillors, 1928. Lye and Wollescote Urban District Council was instituted in 1897 and did much to improve the squalid conditions of the town. Here councillors lead the procession, the highlight of Lye Carnival that year. Behind may be seen Bill Pardoe on his AJS machine, with his beloved future wife Norah in the side-car.

Dr Christopher Darby, 1901. Dr Darby was a GP in Stourbridge Road. He was also Medical Officer of Health on the Council, an ardent supporter of St John's Ambulance Brigade, and a pioneer in new medical treatments.

Edwin Morris, Mayor of Lampeter, 1942.
Edwin was born at his father's jeweller's
shop in Stourbridge Road in 1894. He was
professor of Hebrew and Theology at
Lampeter College, and went on to become
Archbishop of Wales from 1957 to 1971.

Ernest Stevens opening Lye and Wollescote
Park, 9 July 1932. Mr Stevens was a local
industrialist and a great benefactor to the
area. In 1930 he purchased Wollescote Hall
and 89 acres of land adjoining it, which he
gave to the people of Lye for ever. Here
Mr Folkes, Surveyor to the Council, is
presenting Mr Stevens with a gold key to
unlock the main gates.

A Lavender wedding, *c.* 1898. John Lavender, the Lye fishmonger, on the right and his wife Emily Jane, seated left, pose for the camera with the bride, Emily's sister, and her bridegroom. John had five brothers and three sisters; the man on the left is one of his brothers. Meshak Lavender, who owned a high-class tailoring establishment in the High Street, was another brother.

Pardoe wedding, 17 April 1939. The union of two Lye dynasties took place when Colin Pardoe, son of Major Pardoe, head of Crabbe Street School (left), married Madge Round, daughter of Philip Round, Lye industrialist (right). The bridesmaid is Phyllis Round and best man Mr Boyd Weaver. The ceremony was at Pedmore church and was performed by the Rev. Mr Waring.

Mr and Mrs Johnson, 1906. The young bride and groom are Sarah Jane Fisher and Albert Johnson. Albert was a hairdresser and owner of Stambermill post office. A bad heart saved him from military service in 1914, but as his contribution to the war effort he went each Thursday to Studley Court (now part of Mary Stevens Park, Stourbridge), then a military hospital, to shave the wounded soldiers. So horrific were some of the injuries he saw he came home ill every time. He died in his late 30s leaving his wife with five young children and a business to run – in the days of no state aid. She was so successful that all five children (four sons and one daughter, Clarice) became successful members of the community.

Somewhere in wartime Lye, three wedding guests pose outside a heavily sand-bagged building. It is possibly Lye library, as St John's Wesleyan church was next door. The trio are Minnie Taylor on the right, Freddie Handley in the middle and Kathleen ? on the left.

Weston family wedding, 1946. The Westons were a very old Lye family and prominent local shopkeepers. This is the marriage of Anne Weston and Horace Haynes, extreme left on the front row. Beside them are Harold Weston and 'Granny' Weston. In the middle row, left to right, are Bill Weston, Leslie Weston and Vic Weston. The three ladies above, left to right, are Gladys Weston, Lily Weston and Alice Weston.

The wedding of Joe Taylor and Pearl Mullett, September 1945. Joe from the Dock and Pearl from Brierley Hill were both members of Lye Primitive Methodist church. Joe obtained coupons so that Pearl and the bridesmaids could have traditional dresses and Lye shopkeepers helped with reception provisions. Three ministers took part in the ceremony at Brierley Hill Methodist church, and the organist was Donald Richards. On the group photograph with the bride and groom are, left to right, best man Denys Brooks, bridesmaids Nellie Mullett, Daisy, Joe's sister, and Brenda Mullett. Mr Mullett is on the extreme right.

Mathilda Hart, *c.* 1930. Mathilda, born 1871, married Samuel Hart in September 1890. She is photographed with her husband's prize pumpkin, resplendent on a velvet-covered table.

Samuel Hart, *c.* 1930. Born in 1869, he was descended from an old Lye family which can trace its ancestry back for over 250 years. He was a miner and coal merchant, but his chief claim to fame was his growing of prize pumpkins. Eventually the secret of his success was discovered; they were fed on the contents of the cess pit.

Dorothy Howell, FRAM, 1919. Dorothy (see page 27) is shown seated at her piano in Wollescote House. Because she was a famous musician, the family entertained many celebrities including Sir Henry Wood. However, Dorothy remained very level-headed and never forgot her Black Country connections. She often repeated with genuine pleasure 'the opportunities she has had of playing to packed halls full of miners and chain-makers with their wives, and sometimes even with babies in their arms, in the Black Country. They will listen with great attention to a long and serious work . . . and express their pleasure at its close, with thunderous applause' (*Yorkshire Post*, 20 August 1923).

The Hill sisters, mid-1930s. The sisters belonged to an old and distinguished Lye family and were related to Thomas Hill who built Lye church. They themselves were all successful businesswomen. Here, they surround their brother Ernest. Back row, left to right: Bella Simpkiss of the 'Mercy Bar, Nora Holden, antique dealer, Rene Salter, publican, Clara Hall, who helped Maggie, Maggie Wooldridge, who owned two shops – Maggie's in Talbot Street, Lye and Margaret's in Stourbridge; Minnie also assisted her. Front row: Nellie Bedford, of Bedford's fencing, and Florence, who kept a draper's shop. Their father was 'Gentleman John', who always wore a buttonhole and had a little dog. He was involved in gambling and cock-fighting and never seemed to work.

The Pearson family, 1970. Left to right: May (née Pearson), daughter Freda Webb, Alice Pearson and Albert Pearson. Albert was President and Secretary of Lye and Wollescote Pigeon Club for forty-nine years, resigning in 1980. The club was based first at the Seven Stars, Pedmore Road and then the Holly Bush. Alice may also be seen on page 77. She had a long association with the Trade Union movement and the Labour Party. The family kept a shop on the corner of Hill Street and Bank Street and lived in Balds Lane.

Two young soldiers, *c.* 1914. They were photographed by William Pardoe while on leave from the front during the First World War. On the left is Henry Skidmore; on the right his cousin Harry Amphlett. Unlike many of their Lye friends they survived the war.

POWs, Kassel, Germany, 1917. Cecil Lavender is third from the left on the back row. He volunteered in 1914, joining the Northumberland Fusiliers, and in 1915 was in France. Shot in the stomach, he returned to England but then returned for duty. He was again badly wounded by an exploding shell in a trench raid in 1917. The greatest shock was not the possibility of losing a leg but that the stretcher bearer who hauled him out was German. When his captors realised he was a musician he was allowed to entertain senior German officers and local dignitaries. After the war he went north to pursue a distinguished career as professional musician, composer and conductor.

Percy Clewes, *c.* 1914. Percy is photographed here at Caterham Camp in the uniform of the Coldstream Guards. Wounded on the Somme, he was evacuated to London. While recuperating he successfully answered an advert for singers when the chorus of the West End show *Chu Chin Chow* went on strike. He was later sent back to France.

Don Millward, 1939. Don is here a young volunteer at the outbreak of the Second World War. He was evacuated from Dunkirk, only to be caught in the London bombing. The trauma so affected his nerves that he was invalided out on a pension of £1 per week. This was stopped after a year when he was certified fit to work. However, he never fully recovered, and said the experience taught him never to volunteer for anything in future!

Marjorie Stanley, *c.* 1933. Marjorie showed exceptional promise as a ballet and ballroom dancer at a very early age and won many awards. As a very young woman she opened her own dancing schools, and has enjoyed a long and successful career in her profession.

Taylor family, 1974. Back row, left to right: Stan, Bill and Vernon. Front row: Harold, Priscilla and Laura. These same brothers and sisters are shown some sixty years earlier on page 35; in this photograph they are celebrating Priscilla's golden wedding. Her husband was Dick, member of the well-known Rhodes family of Lye.

Polly Skidmore, 1920s: a fitting photograph with which to end this book and with it a story which is typical of the kindness of the old Lye folk. Polly brought up her sister Alice's six children when Alice, wife of Percy Clewes, died at the age of 36. Polly had two children of her own but treated all alike, and they all loved her.

ACKNOWLEDGEMENTS

D. Allcock, H. Attwood, M. Ayres, F. Bache, Ben Baker's, S. Bevan, *The Blackcountryman* magazine, John Cooksey, R. Cooper, A. Crowe, M. Davies, S. Fletcher, A. Fox, Robert Frogatt, Mrs C. Gadd, D. Griffiths, F. Guest, J. Haden, Mr and Mrs Hart, Billy Hart, P. Hayward, Mr and Mrs Heathcote, Helix Ltd, P. Hickman, Mr and Mrs Hill, Stan Hill, M. Howell, Howell Family Trust, Mr and Mrs T. Jones, C. Lavender, J. Lavender, B. Layland, C. Lees, F. Lowe, Mrs Millward, J. Morris, David Pardoe, Len Pardoe, R. Pardoe, N. Pearsall, Mr Pearson, D. Pearson, L. Perks, Mrs S. Roberts, Pearl Taylor, Sybil Taylor, Mrs Turner, Mrs Usherwood, H. Walton M. Wassell, F. Webb, R. Wilkes, H. Worton.

Sincere apologies if anyone has been omitted.

The Brettell family, *c.* 1900. This was a well-known Lye family. Back row, left to right: David Brettell, Jane Brettell, Mary Foxall, Emily Dickens, William Brettell, Priscilla Hollyoak, Howard Brettell. Front row: Sarah Pardoe, Rosanna Brettell, Absolom Brettell, Rose Bridgewater.